TRAVELS WITH CHECKPOINTS

ORAN BURKE

Travels with Checkpoints

Copyright © Oran Burke 2012

Published by ORBB

www.oranburke.com

www.facebook.com/travelswithcheckpoints

First published September 2012

This edition published May 2013

Oran Burke has asserted his right under the Copyright, Designs and Patents Act 1988 to be identified as author of this work

All rights reserved. No part of this publication may be reproduced, distributed, or transmitted in any form or by any means, including photocopying, recording, or other electronic or mechanical methods, without the prior written permission of the publisher, except in the case of brief quotations embodied in critical reviews and certain other non-commercial uses permitted by copyright law.

Cover photo © Colm Burke

Cover design by Jess Hillier

ISBN 978-0-9572689-0-6

*For police and border guards everywhere,
may they be happy in their work.*

CONTENTS

INTRODUCTION	7
UZBEKISTAN, AUGUST 2005	11
KYRGYZSTAN, SEPTEMBER 2005	39
CUBA, EARLY 2007	51
ECUADOR, SEPTEMBER 2010	61
BOLIVIA, DECEMBER 2010	79
AND FINALLY...	91

Introduction

There is no better feeling than the beginning - that point after making a decision, storing my worldly goods, packing a rucksack and landing somewhere I've never been before. There may be months stretching ahead to plod along at whatever pace I choose, stopping if I like a place, moving on if I don't. A lack of planning only adds to the anticipation, allowing a random meander and the ability to discover places in my own time. It takes a few days to adjust to the time zone, a week or so to the idea that I don't have to deal with normal day to day life, and a month or two before truly relaxing.

My personal travel addiction is the long overland journey, although the need to work and save means these only happen every few years. With nothing to do for five to fifty hours but sit and wait to arrive, there's a lot of time to think, read a book or just stare out the window. There are certainly dull periods, but drifting slowly across huge land masses like Asia or South America without flying offers a different perspective. It's easier to see the gradual changes in people, language and landscape, and while political lines mark the separation of states, geography and culture tend to be less fussy.

This method of travelling can involve passing through a lot of checkpoints and borders, and it's here that contact with various officials from the police, army or immigration takes place. Most of these meetings pass quietly and without incident, but always with the mutual acceptance that you could be held there for no particular reason, and the level of bureaucracy experienced can be a good indicator of the stability of a state, its authoritarianism or paranoia.

I love borders in their most basic form, a crossing point from one country to another. They can be frenzied, calm, part of large towns, remote outposts or physically defined by rivers or mountains. A mixed collection of people converge on the same point to funnel through to the other side for whatever their reason is that day. However, there are also times when you wish you'd chosen a different route. Being tall, Irish and genetically pale makes me stand out from the crowd and, very occasionally, attract attention that isn't always welcome.

Most of these stories involve my seemingly unwavering ability to get into situations involving representatives of some of the states I've passed through. I can't claim that it's never my fault, as I've often made the mistakes that caused the problems, but in my defence, it's impossible to know everything about a country before you arrive. Over time I haven't lost this talent; I've just gotten better at negotiating my way out.

Much of this can be put down to attempts at communication. While it's not possible to learn every language, a few basic words and a lot of hand gestures can go a long way. Most of the conversations in the following pages are based on this linguistic system, translated into English. It's hard to get a flavour of a country without learning something about its people, and the only way to do this is to try and speak. Also, this has provided a basic level of protection more times than I can remember. Almost everyone I've met didn't try to rob me, instead tending to be curious and helpful, providing an added layer of guidance you otherwise might not have. This can often lead to the same conversation about where you're from and what you're doing there, but small talk can lead to bigger talk.

Uzbekistan, August 2005

I'd travelled from Istanbul to Iran with an old friend who then left to meet his girlfriend in Dubai. We arranged to meet up in Tashkent, the capital of Uzbekistan, ten days later to continue our journey along parts of the Silk Road, the network of ancient intercontinental trade routes that once linked Asia, Africa and Europe. The first thing that became apparent when we started out in Turkey was the bureaucracy that the Central Asian states would inflict on us. Having been created in Stalin's time, effectively as provinces run by Moscow and part of the USSR until its dissolution, the paperwork needed to enter them didn't seem to have changed since that era. I'd gotten my Uzbek visa in Ankara on the second attempt, as an error in the embassy took two weeks to uncover. I needed a letter of invitation, a puzzling system which involves somebody in a travel agency, who doesn't know you, writing a letter inviting you to come to the country. You never see any of the paperwork, but it results in the embassy realising that you should, after all, be given a visa.

This was the beginning of the most unknown part of the trip, a long haul through Turkmenistan, Uzbekistan, Tajikistan, Kyrgyzstan and a little bit of Kazakhstan (it's very big). The police in this region had a reputation for hassling foreign visitors for bribes, although rumours at the time indicated this wasn't as severe a problem as it had once been. Some countries had opened up to tourism, while others had developed their oil and gas industries, so the authorities were becoming more used to outsiders. Having travelled through Iran, where any preconceptions we had were dismantled by the engaging warmth we encountered, it was easy to see how the day to day realities of a country could be misrepresented by concentrating solely on the actions of a government. In the month we were there – captivated by a unique culture, sweltering in the humidity of the Persian Gulf or awestruck by the lunar-like landscape of the eastern desert – we slowly and unavoidably readjusted our views of a place that made the news for all the wrong reasons. I hoped the affectionately named "Stans" of Central Asia would be the same.

Travels with Checkpoints

Travelling over the mountain range that separated Iran from Turkmenistan, I was in a cheery, mildly anxious mood. The country was known for having a North Korean style of government where President Sapurmarat Niyazov, the former leader of the Turkmen Communist Party, had stayed in power and adapted the country to his needs following the break-up of the Soviet Union. Among many other things, he rewrote the nation's history to include himself as Turkmenbashi, Leader of all Turkmen, renamed the months of the year and built huge marble ministries while much of the population survived on a few dollars a day. A seventy metre column in the capital Ashgabat was topped by a gold statue of him, arms outstretched and inviting praise, which rotated to face the sun during the day.

This cult of personality was everywhere you went, but it was less than fifteen years since the country had defaulted into independence, and the generation who'd grown up before his omnipotence didn't seem so keen on his version of events. A tour of a museum one day reinforced this, as all the exhibits included a section on the self-proclaimed President for Life which my guide, a well educated historian, passed over without comment.

It was mandatory to buy a guided tour to visit the country to ensure you were chaperoned from one government approved place to another, but there was a loophole. A transit visa allowed you to travel unaccompanied along a roughly predefined route, your options limited by the fact that there were only three or four main roads crossing the country. You had to declare your entry and exit points and get from A to B in the time you'd been allocated. It had all the qualities of a somewhat surreal reality TV show, in which you had to spot as many peculiarities as you could while racing to exit the country before the propaganda grappled you to the ground. I chose to enter near Ashgabat and leave from Turkmenabat and was given five days, enough for an afternoon in the capital, two nights in the central town of Mary exploring the nearby ruins of the Silk Road city of Merv, and travel time to get me to the border before my visa ran out. It turned out to be a great way to negotiate the country, journeying from the capital across the gritty Karakum desert to the green north-eastern edges.

I travelled in minibuses, which allowed me more contact with the constantly friendly Turkmens. My phrasebook was permanently to hand, even if most conversations involved pointing rather than speaking. At the regular checkpoints a window would often be slid open from the outside, and an official-looking hand would appear to which a pile of passports would be offered. My fellow passengers would often stop me giving mine when I didn't need to. When there was contact with the police, usually at isolated provincial borders where registration was compulsory, the driver always came with me, making sure everything was reported correctly. I can't say if all this protected me from the attentions of the police or not, but it certainly made me trust the Turkmen people.

The morning I left for Uzbekistan I was relaxed. The helpful minibus driver that had taken me from Mary to Turkmenabat the day before had pointed out where to get shared taxis to the border. These were a common mode of transport in Central Asia where you turned up, agreed a price with the driver and waited for the other seats in the car to fill. This could take ten minutes or three hours and you might share with three large men or a little old lady, the difference between comfort and half-hourly exercises in shifting your arse, legs and feet by the miniscule amounts needed to avoid numbness.

I set off before seven as I was due in Tashkent that night and it was still six hundred kilometres, several modes of transport and a border crossing away. The taxi stop was across from my hotel so I wandered over to find a lift to the frontier, a forty five minute drive away. I arrived at the same time as an army officer and four young soldiers, who didn't appear to take much notice of me. The officer was short and stout, dressed smartly in a cream uniform with a peaked cap. The soldiers, who couldn't have been more than eighteen, were marginally less well clad, wearing brown sackcloth-style uniforms and no hats. A family piling into a car invited me to join them. It would have been a squeeze but they looked like good company for the journey, so I started to walk towards them until there was a slight change of atmosphere. The driver was avoiding eye contact and everyone else looked unsure. I couldn't understand what was going on as they left without me, and another man grabbed my arm and dragged me towards his cab.

Confused by the early hour and what had just happened I accepted his price, a little more than I should have paid, threw my backpack in the boot and jumped in the passenger seat. The four soldiers then occupied the back seat of the car. The driver must have seen the look of alarm on my face as he attempted to indicate, through smiles and hand gestures, that all of this was fine and normal. The officer wanted a free lift for his troops, and I was the one chosen to pay. There wasn't much I could do about it, so I settled in and answered their questions about where I was from and what I was doing there. For some unknown reason, they chose not to speak directly to me, instead channelling their questions through the driver, who didn't speak any English either. He would then answer them with the words I spoke, which would be met with wise nods and mild exclamations.

They got out at a checkpoint about fifteen minutes later, and we carried on, passing through vast fields of surprisingly scratchy looking cotton plants, irrigated by one of Central Asia's once mighty rivers, the

Amu Darya, historically called the Oxus. Soon after, we crept across this wide, lazy waterway on a trembling pontoon bridge; a few weeks later I saw it again as it trickled towards the desert that used to be the southern Aral Sea, heavily depleted by the thirsty crops upstream.

When we arrived at the end of the road, the remote, calmly chaotic border was still closed. There were people ten deep in front of a wood frame and barbed wire gate, waiting patiently to leave. I hung around at the back and passed the time chatting to some English guys who were doing the Mongol Rally, an annual race from London to Mongolia in a small car of your choice. I also changed some money into Uzbek Som and worked out that I would probably have enough to get to Bukhara, the nearest town on the other side; from there I would hop in a shared taxi to Tashkent, theoretically leaving me with enough small change to get the Metro close to the hotel where I'd agreed to meet my friend. I also had an emergency twenty dollar note in a hidden pocket, should this perfect plan fail.

Eventually two Turkmen soldiers appeared and surveyed the crowd. One of them spotted the English guys and me, indicating we should come forward. The blockade parted and we advanced to the gate. It opened, our documents were checked and we were moved on to the small immigration post. This special treatment obviously went against my European standards of fair play, but in the interests of diplomacy I kept my complaints to myself. Having answered a couple of gentle questions about where I'd stayed and the route I'd taken, I walked on alone while the rally team sorted out their paperwork.

Uzbekistan was one of the countries that had needed a backup plan. In May the security services had opened fire on a group of protesters in the eastern town of Andijan. The estimated death toll was generally considered to have been significantly higher than the official government figure of 187. Islam Karimov, the president since independence from Russia in the early 1990s, responded to international condemnation by ignoring it. Since then there had been no other trouble that we knew of, but there was no reason to be complacent. We'd kept a watchful eye on news reports, ready to bypass it if necessary.

The Uzbek side of the frontier consisted of a couple of small prefabricated huts and a bigger structure that looked like a school gym. As I passed the door of the first cabin, a slim well dressed man in civilian clothes glanced at me and said, "Tourist? Come here, medical check". Once inside, he informed me that he was the doctor, took my passport and wrote the details in a ledger. He then turned to me and, with a casual sweeping movement of his hand in my direction, said, "Everything ok?" Answering yes was all that was needed for the precious medical stamp on my passport, something I was never asked to show again. Interestingly, I never met anyone else who had to go through this intense, invasive examination either.

I walked on, bemused, to where a soldier stood behind a table surrounded by people. Having been first through the gate and only spent about a minute in the doctor's office, I couldn't understand where they'd all come from. I stopped and he handed me two copies of a form. I'd filled out many of these customs declarations over the years and had found that they were normally taken from you, put in a pile and rarely looked at. I filled them in without paying too much attention to detail, partly because it was written in Cyrillic so I couldn't understand much of it. The only obvious part was the money section as it had a dollar sign beside it, and it was here I made the decision that was to drag my day down not once, but twice.

The embargo on some financial institutions operating in Iran meant it wasn't possible to use international credit cards, so I'd brought a lot of cash in dollars and euros. I had more than was needed so there was plenty left over, safely hidden on my person. I also had some traveller's cheques, but wasn't sure exactly how many, so used the same system I had when entering Turkmenistan. I underestimated, more to appear like I had less than to smuggle, as I didn't want to attract the attention of border guards once notorious for shaking down foreigners. I assumed it wouldn't make a difference, as I'd be waved through to enjoy the delights Uzbekistan had to offer.

I entered the main building which inside looked like a passport control area from any border, a large hall with four booths where the immigration officers should have been. Instead, there was just one young guy, dressed in a dark green uniform, standing behind a table next to a room with the only sign in English I'd seen so far – PRIVATE EXAMINATION ROOM. He took my documents, surveyed them briefly, pointed at the number I'd written down and asked me to show him the money. I held out, as I didn't like the idea of revealing where my valuables were hidden. Eventually bowing to the inevitable, I hesitantly put my hand down my pants and pulled my money belt out of its home in my underwear. Suspiciously, I handed over all my currency and traveller's cheques.

He counted the cash, then held up the form and said, "Dollar." I was puzzled as, although I knew there was going to be a difference between the amount declared and the total on the table, I wasn't holding anything back. He decided to up the level of questioning, tapping me sharply on the chest while repeating his "Dollar" mantra. I continued to point at the scattered pile on the table each time he did this. I made a more accurate calculation of how much there was and it was about a thousand dollars more than written down. This wasn't going well, so I fell back on the less than noble method of acting like I didn't understand which was mostly true as he seemed to be asking me for extra.

Eventually, he got bored, as I couldn't produce something I didn't have. He spoke into his radio and a soldier arrived to take my passport away, which I wasn't overly happy about. I usually prefer to keep it close when travelling, like an internationally recognized security blanket. Next, another young guy in uniform and the doctor turned up. Having a medical examiner present didn't necessarily bode well, and he was the first to talk, asking if I spoke English. My spirits lifted as I knew I'd be able to sort all this out if I could communicate, so I answered with a resoundingly positive "Yes!" He grunted, sat down and started counting the money.

After a few more awkward minutes standing around in silence, another man in a dark green uniform joined us. I discovered later that this colour ensemble was usually worn by the police, and I can only assume that this was who I was dealing with as they never introduced themselves properly. The latest arrival took over the interrogation as he spoke fluent English. Ominously, he reminded me of the Turkmen army officer who'd requisitioned my car earlier, but with an extra pinch of stereotyping. He was small, round and balding with chubby, nicotine-stained fingers and yellowy-black teeth.

When he spoke, the cliché was quickly banished. He questioned me forensically about where the rest of the money was, and it seemed that being able to speak my native language might not help after all. For five minutes he asked the same question and I gave the same answer, until I discovered what was causing the confusion. They didn't seem to know what traveller's cheques were and assumed I had more cash. I explained how they worked but this didn't help. He told me that under Uzbek law, he could confiscate the surplus, which he then counted out – US$700, €200 and a US$100 cheque. I could go to a judge in Tashkent and try to claim my money back if I thought it had been taken without justification, though I was fairly sure this wouldn't be worth pursuing.

I was now surrounded by three police officers and a doctor, who was still mesmerised by the cash, picking it up now and again to count and caress it, as if he wanted to go somewhere private and roll around on a bed with it. All the funds for the rest of my trip were on the table and even though it was my own fault, I wasn't eager to lose such a large chunk. I was aware that this was a particularly tempting amount for the men around me, but the more I heard about confiscation and courts, the more I could see they didn't want that. I was probably in the wrong from a legal point of view, but they still hadn't seized the money and given me a receipt I could take to a judge. What they really wanted was for me to offer them something and everything would have been conveniently forgotten.

It was time for a last desperate attempt at defence, so I mentioned that I couldn't read the form properly. When this was translated, the doctor groaned and stood up to leave, arms held up in exasperation, until my interpreter said something and he sat down again, like a solo Mexican wave. I wasn't panicking but my situation clearly wasn't good. I debated with him for another ten minutes until it seemed like I should probably give up. My only advantage was that there would never be a straight request for a bribe, as that would somehow break the unofficial rules of engagement.

They started to search my backpack, a measure designed to increase the pressure. It worked as I was now answering questions while trying to watch as the others, all three of them, rifled through my belongings. First out was a bag of medicines I was keeping for my friend. He hadn't wanted to bring them to Dubai where they might not have been legal. What are the questions you get asked anytime you board a flight? Are you carrying anything for anyone else? Did you pack this bag yourself? They took a great interest in them until the doctor had a look and shrugged his shoulders. So far, my experiences with him suggested this wouldn't be the best place to fall ill.

I was asked for my passport and instantly and unintentionally showed that the stress was getting to me. I whined that someone had taken it away, and I'm sure I saw a flicker of pity cross my interrogator's face. He then said he wasn't sure how we were going to solve this problem, and that he was going to have to call his superior.

A small man with a moustache had been loitering at the other end of the hall for the last ten minutes, watching without getting involved, and he was now called over. He had a kindly face but it didn't improve my circumstances as there were now five people to pay off. I only had hundred dollar bills so it could have been expensive. I began to wonder whether asking for change would have been rude.

When everything had been explained to him, my conversation with the boss went something like this.

Boss (with large smile): "Tourist?"

Me (with large forced smile): "Yes."

Boss (pointing in the direction I was now desperate to head): "Bukhara, Samarkand?"

Me (smiling hopefully): "Yes!"

I have no idea what he said next as it was in Uzbek, but he said it with a smile on his face, so I've always imagined it was "Have a lovely time in our country."

He then turned to the other four and snarled; the doctor and the second guard disappeared rapidly; the boss smiled, shook my hand and wandered off.

I was told I could go, but to not make any more mistakes during my time in Uzbekistan. I was asked to count my money to make sure it was all there, and my passport complete with entry stamp miraculously reappeared. I gathered my belongings, feeling partially dazed at the abrupt ending, and walked out of the immigration hall, never looking back. It was a hundred metres to where transport left for Bukhara, but it felt like much longer.

I'd managed to get away without paying, but this wasn't the time for celebration. I wanted to get in a taxi and speed away from there. Unfortunately, the elderly gentleman I chose drove a car which had seen better centuries, moving so slowly that the border seemed to be catching up with us. I think he sensed my nervous agitation, probably because I kept looking over my shoulder, and not long into the journey he flagged down a more modern car. After some roadside negotiation he told me to swap over. There was a short discussion about paying the money in advance, which I refused. They accepted they could sort it out between themselves, I got in the other car and the frontier finally began to fade.

My new driver was a young, talkative guy, and we discussed family and travels on the way into town, passing through drier countryside than on the Turkmen side. I began to relax, and a short half hour later we were on the outskirts of Bukhara. As we passed through a checkpoint, a young policeman in a now recognizable uniform saw me and stopped the car. My passport was requested and when he opened it, my copy of the customs form was folded inside. I'd been so anxious to get away I hadn't thought to hide it and he had a quick look before deciding to search my luggage. Under the bag of medicines he found two books – a novel and a history tome. I'd apparently made another mistake. There was a section for listing any printed material you had, in case any of them happened to be banned by the government. I'd left it blank because, until that moment, I hadn't understood what it was. While the books were unlikely to be illegal, not declaring them was a problem. He signalled for me to follow him and the taxi driver began to argue on my behalf. I was extremely grateful, but knew he wasn't going to win. He was told to get back in his car and wait.

Across the road was a small round building that looked like a concrete yurt, common at checkpoints in Uzbekistan. I reluctantly shuffled towards it, past another policeman lazing under an umbrella. The one room inside was about four metres in diameter, furnished with a desk and two chairs. Strangely, these weren't arranged in the traditional manner common in most parts of the world; one seat was on the floor but the other was upright on top of the desk, facing you as you walked in. My tired, frayed mind imagined terrible visions of unusual torture methods, though it also occurred to me that they might have been playing musical chairs.

He put the books on the desk and for the second time in an hour I was in the hands of an Uzbek official who was telling me I'd committed a crime, but wasn't taking out a notepad to issue a fine. My only advantage this time was that neither of us spoke the other's language. He told me to empty my pockets which contained, among other things, the small amount of local currency I'd changed. If he took this I would probably have been stuck in Bukhara for the night, searching for a moneychanger. Weirdly, he didn't seem interested in it, instead jabbing the customs form with his finger and saying something in Uzbek. I replied in English that I didn't understand. This continued for a minute or so until, fed up of the game, he held up the piece of paper and shouted,

"Dollar!" It was the larger amount of cash he wanted to see, which was safely back in my pants.

Even now I'm not sure where the next word came from. I may have been emboldened by my previous escape, or delirious from my morning's experiences. I stood firm, shook my head and said, "No". He looked shocked but quickly regained his composure. Sternly, he pointed at the form and said, "Dollar". I pointed in the direction of the border and said that everything was ok at customs, hoping he wouldn't contact them. We repeated this a few times until he tired of it and began to inspect the picture page of my passport. I pointed at the word Ireland and asked about calling my embassy. There wasn't an Irish embassy in Uzbekistan but I was betting that he wasn't going to phone them.

The gamble seemed to work, or he just got bored of me as he said I could go. I put everything back in my pockets but as I reached for the offending books he tried to stop me. For some reason he wanted to keep them, but again I said no, picked them up and walked towards the door. He may have been a little surprised that someone had stood up to him, probably not common in Uzbekistan. I left with everything I came in with, bar the sweat of stress, and walked back to the taxi, leaving a bewildered policeman behind me. I wonder if he went back to the station later and told his colleagues about the one that got away.

My driver looked sympathetically embarrassed, and as we drove away held his hand up in the international sign for money, rubbing his fingers and thumb together. He also raised an eyebrow and I rightly deduced this to be a question about whether I'd paid a bribe. I smiled and said no; he looked astonished, then pleased, and shook my hand. Whether or not it was still commonplace for foreigners to be targeted, it seemed Uzbeks were fully aware of the capabilities of their police force. That he had chosen to argue, if only for thirty seconds, was impressive.

When we arrived at Bukhara bus station, it was a few kilometres outside the town centre and had no banks. I'd paid for the taxi with my emergency twenty dollars and even though I had several hundred-denomination notes in dollars and euros, this wasn't going to get me to the capital as drivers wouldn't be able to change them. It had been a long morning and it was now after midday, so the next five minutes would be crucial to my mood. If I had enough money to get to Tashkent, I was prepared to go hungry for the seven hours it would take to get there. If not, I'd grab a hotel and continue in the morning, though my preference was definitely to carry on and meet my friend. I approached the next driver in the queue and he offered me a price that matched my ever decreasing budget, with enough left over to get the Metro at the other end and possibly buy a little food. I agreed and we waited for the car to fill.

Ten minutes later we set off with only three of the four places filled, and twenty minutes into the journey stopped to eat. Over lunch it became clear that they wanted me to pay extra for the empty seat, and that the other passengers were going to share the cost so we could travel more spaciously. This turned out to be fairly common in parts of Central Asia and I always assumed it was a ruse to get a bit more cash from tourists. I had no choice but to say no, a word I was beginning to associate with this country. I showed them I had only enough money to pay the original price and for the food I was eating, a tasteless meat-filled pastry parcel. They then asked if I had any "Dollar", another question I was getting used to hearing.

I may have misplaced my sense of humour at this point, as they dropped the subject and then did something which, like the previous guy arguing with the policeman, helped moderate some of the dire opinions I was developing. The driver paid for my meal, refusing to take anything from me. I was to learn over the next few months that this sort of hospitality was commonplace in the region. I could have paid but he saw I was having a bad day, and the Uzbek instinct was to welcome and take care of visitors. He still stopped five minutes later to pick up a fourth passenger, but now that just made me smile.

The journey to Tashkent crossed wide, grassy plains, dotted here and there with run down agro-industrial complexes, before ending on the outskirts of the city just before dark. I had a few coins remaining to get to the hotel, and I was tired. The policeman in the metro who checked my passport was swiftly dealt with, leaving me to marvel wearily at the city's occasionally ostentatious underground system. Built by the Russians, artistry and engineering mixed comfortably. It was designed to withstand earthquakes with many stations doubling as Cold War nuclear bunkers, and the decoration of each stop was unique. That evening however, I may not have appreciated its full majesty.

I got to the hotel an hour or so later to discover they'd never heard of my friend. They were also full. Exhaustion started to bear down hard on me as I wandered around searching for a room for the night. Everywhere seemed to be occupied but I eventually found a warm, friendly place down a side street. It cost much more than I'd hoped but they accepted my credit card, normally reserved for emergencies. I showered, cashed some precious traveller's cheques and found an internet cafe. I located my friend in another place around the corner; he'd left a message but it had gotten lost during a shift change. More than fifteen hours after starting my journey, I sat down with a large gin and tonic and told him the story of my day.

After a good meal, a beer or two and a decent night's sleep, it was easier to see the funny side, but I was cautious. Over the next few weeks document checks were common, and having to walk through three lines of truncheon wielding policemen to see a football match almost gave me palpitations. Nevertheless, the country was historically intriguing and the people curious and welcoming. The constant invitations for dinner were often overwhelming, especially an hour or two after meeting someone. Initially viewed with some suspicion, it quickly became normal and unthreatening, and by the time we left my wariness was reserved exclusively for the state.

Travels with Checkpoints

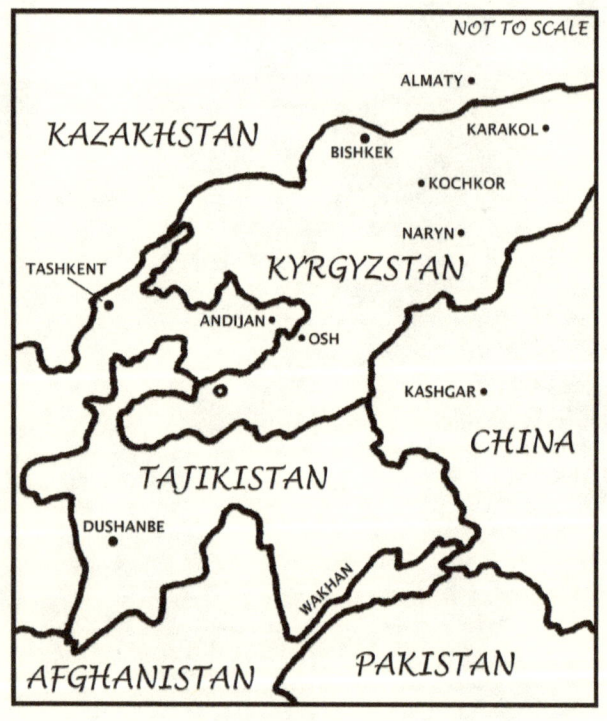

Kyrgyzstan, September 2005

After Uzbekistan we passed through Tajikistan, where I retained a healthy nervousness at the numerous checkpoints. It was a beautiful and sparse country, especially in the eastern Gorno-Badakshan region where the Pamir mountain range offered an ever-changing panorama of colours. We were required to register almost everywhere, especially in the Wakhan Valley which bordered Afghanistan. There were some noteworthy occurrences, like being interrogated by the local head of the KGB in one village. We'd gone for a walk by the river which formed the natural border between the two countries and he wanted to know why, a question that baffled us at the time. The further we travelled in this isolated region, the more we became used to the constant stream of soldiers checking bags and documents and, in one curious event in the most remote part of the valley, removing fuel from our jeep, an unusual toll which left our jeep driver having to freewheel down mountain roads to get to our destination.

Next in line was Kyrgyzstan, somewhere we'd also had to monitor closely as, similar to Uzbekistan, there had been recent unrest. The town of Osh in the south was the first place we arrived, close to Jalalabad where trouble had originally flared following a disputed election in March. This had led to an opposition group taking control of the south of the country by storming government buildings. The presidential palace in Bishkek, the capital, was ransacked by protesters soon after, and President Askar Akayev – another leader who had ruled since the fall of the Soviet Union – fled the country amid largely peaceful protests that became known as the Tulip Revolution. Kurmanbek Bakiyev, a former prime minister, had been elected after serving as interim president until elections in July, and the situation seemed to have stabilized.

In late September, having travelled to Karakol in the east, I went south alone to Kochkor, a pleasant market town. The nearby lake of Song-Köl was rumoured to be gorgeous and I'd hoped to do some trekking, something the country was becoming known for, but it was too late in the year. I left and went further south to

Naryn, to do some short walks and visit the ancient caravanserai of Tash Rabat. On the way back north, I stopped again in KochKor, as I'd liked the town and hoped to find someone willing to share a taxi up to the lake for a day trip. I did and it was worth the trip, a high plateau containing a wide lake surrounded by lush green hills. As it was late in the season, nearly all the yak herders who brought their animals there for the summer had left for lower pastures, giving the lake a serene, uncluttered feel. I then hung around the town for a few days, enjoying the off-season emptiness.

One afternoon I went in search of food and found a pleasant restaurant which was entered through a corridor from the main street, walking through to a back room with six or seven tables. It was small and hidden away from the noise of the road, a good place to eat a slow lunch with a book. I was the only person there so I settled in and ordered a bowl of spicy laghman, a thick noodle soup, and a pot of green tea. I had just finished my meal when three men walked in. The first thing I noticed was that two of them were policemen, which tensed me momentarily. The second was that one of them was carrying a half empty bottle of vodka. Central Asia had involved drinking plenty of vodka, the de facto celebratory drink, a legacy of Russian rule in a predominantly Muslim region. When you were a guest it would usually be offered as a toast, generally in a large shot glass but, on more formal occasions, in little bowls full to the brim. It always seemed rude to refuse though sometimes I did, as breakfast just seemed too early. My first thought however had nothing to do with drinking. Kyrgyzstan was arguably the most liberal country in the region and there weren't as many checkpoints. Visitors weren't tracked, giving a greater impression of freedom than other states, and the reputation of the police was far better than its neighbours. I hadn't dealt with them drunk before however.

As they came in I'd made eye contact with the first officer, who said hello in English before sitting down. He had clearly had a few drinks, but was friendly. The second uniformed man, much younger and drunker, pointed at the insignia on his jacket and said, "Politsia", while grinning uncontrollably. The third guy, who wore jeans and a t-shirt, sat down before asking me if I spoke Kyrgyz. He was the largest, six feet tall and stocky, and I hoped saying no didn't offend him. They sat at the table across from me and ordered a tomato salad and some shot glasses. They poured, raised a toast and downed them in one swift motion before turning to speak to me. The older policeman asked me where I was from before asking me to join them. Naturally I hesitated but was eventually persuaded. They didn't seem too menacing, just three guys in the middle of the afternoon sharing a few vodkas and a plate of tomatoes.

Maybe this was what I needed, to sit down and have a pleasant, sociable chat with some local law enforcement officers, see their human side and put my previous problems in the past. I was offered vodka, which I accepted. One wouldn't hurt would it?

Vodka 1: everything was nice and friendly. I can't remember what the compulsory toast was dedicated to, maybe Ireland or Kyrgyzstan. I learnt from our conversation, which took place in broken English and Russian, that I was speaking to a captain and his two deputies, and that there was a policeman's holiday that day. I may not have understood fully but there had been some kind of official ceremony going on earlier in the day so I let it go. Why there was a holiday just for the police, which they had decided to celebrate by wandering drunkenly around town in their uniforms, wasn't a question I wanted to ask.

Vodka 2, five minutes later: when I protested they promised there wouldn't be another, so I agreed. I can't remember what we raised our glasses to, probably Kyrgyzstan or Ireland. The waitress was called over and she sat uneasily for a short while until the younger policeman began to grope her. She left quickly and the captain asked jokingly if I'd like to see her strip. I declined politely. Despite this slightly unsavoury moment I wasn't particularly intimidated and, while these guys were obviously in a position of power, they were being good-natured. I didn't feel like I needed to get up and go, but that if I had tried, they would probably have objected.

Vodka 3, about three minutes later: they promised there wouldn't be another so I agreed. The plainclothes man told me about his daughter who had died. This was sad but also disturbing, as he accompanied the story with actions which mimicked him holding a child on his lap and pointing a gun before pulling the trigger. I genuinely think I hadn't fully understood but the mood around the table became fleetingly unpleasant. The captain told him to shut up and asked me about Irish football (soccer, not the Gaelic variety), a subject I've become expert at discussing in many languages except English.

Vodka 4, five minutes later: they promised there wouldn't be another. I think we toasted Roy Keane. The waitress was watching nervously now and appeared to have called reinforcements. It was a family restaurant, and what looked like her brother, mother and grandmother were standing by the counter watching. The captain and plainclothes guy were both talking at me at the same time. The captain had lost control of his spittle, which landed on my face as he spoke. He was also dribbling a bit. Plainclothes-man was trying to shout over the captain while the younger policeman just sat there smiling drunkenly, sporadically pointing at his lapel and saying "Politsia." I was mostly silent now as opening my mouth would have resulted in a stream of saliva down my throat, and I didn't feel our friendship had reached that level yet.

Vodka 5, about five minutes later: they stopped promising there would be no more and I resigned myself to being stuck there. I was aware that I probably needed to think about an exit strategy. Their new trick was shoving a fork with a slice of tomato down my throat directly after the vodka. This was better than it sounds as it took the edge off the taste, like a lazy Bloody Mary with a dash of discomfort. The conversation was no longer sensible and I noticed there was a bustle amongst the restaurant staff before somebody left through the front entrance. A few minutes later, a bearded man appeared and surveyed the scene before smiling mysteriously and leaving. I assumed he had been summoned to be my saviour but he evidently thought I was okay. We had run out of vodka and it looked like the perfect time to make my excuses and leave, but my new friends had other ideas. A menu appeared and I was offered the opportunity to buy another bottle of vodka, which didn't sound like a good idea. It arrived soon after.

Vodka 6 plus tomato: I'd been sitting with them for about half an hour and I was definitely drunk. The old lady I'd earlier assumed was the grandmother, a small, plump lady of about seventy, arrived at the table and spoke harshly to the policemen. I couldn't understand what was said but they looked worried. Until then, I hadn't considered a bad ending; the captain seemed genuine, the young guy was too drunk to do anything other than point out he was a policeman and although plainclothes man was mildly aggressive he had been kept under control. Nonetheless, when she turned to me and pointed at my original table, I got up and prepared to leave. The captain kept saying "Oran, friend, sit" but she was standing between us, refusing to move. Eventually, under pressure, she gave up, and I was dragged back into my seat. The warm fuzzy feeling that six large shots of vodka had given me was fading fast.

Vodka 7, more tomato shoved in my mouth: The young guy from the restaurant, who I'd assumed was the grandson, turned out to speak fluent English. He came to the table and said, "Excuse me, do you want to sit with these people?" I wasn't sure how to answer but my hesitation wasn't important – the old lady reappeared and kicked the policemen out. The captain and young guy left quickly, escorted by Grandma.

Mr. Plainclothes loitered and moved more slowly towards the door. He was carrying the remaining half bottle of vodka and offered it to me. I was happy to accept but he didn't just hand it over, he tried to open my bag to put it inside. I had heard several stories about policemen pretending to search your backpack to see if there was anything they could rob, so I stood there trying to stop him. It must have looked amusing as I twisted my body away from him and he danced drunkenly around me, grabbing at the strap of my bag and eventually winning the handbag battle. He must have been disappointed to find a guide book, a novel and some toilet roll, because he shoved the bottle into my hand and walked off in a huff.

I was told to stay in the restaurant and I passed the time by going to the toilet, an outhouse across some waste ground to the side of the building. There was a dog lying by the door which ignored me but started to bark wildly while I was inside. When I came out I saw why, plainclothes was trying to climb the fence leading to where I was, presumably to try and get to me, giving up when he was spotted from the restaurant. The family were watching from the front door and a few minutes later I was told to come out and walk the opposite direction from the police. As I wobbled off the grandson said, "Our police are crazy, be careful, they might try to steal your money." I made a fuzzy mental note to take his advice.

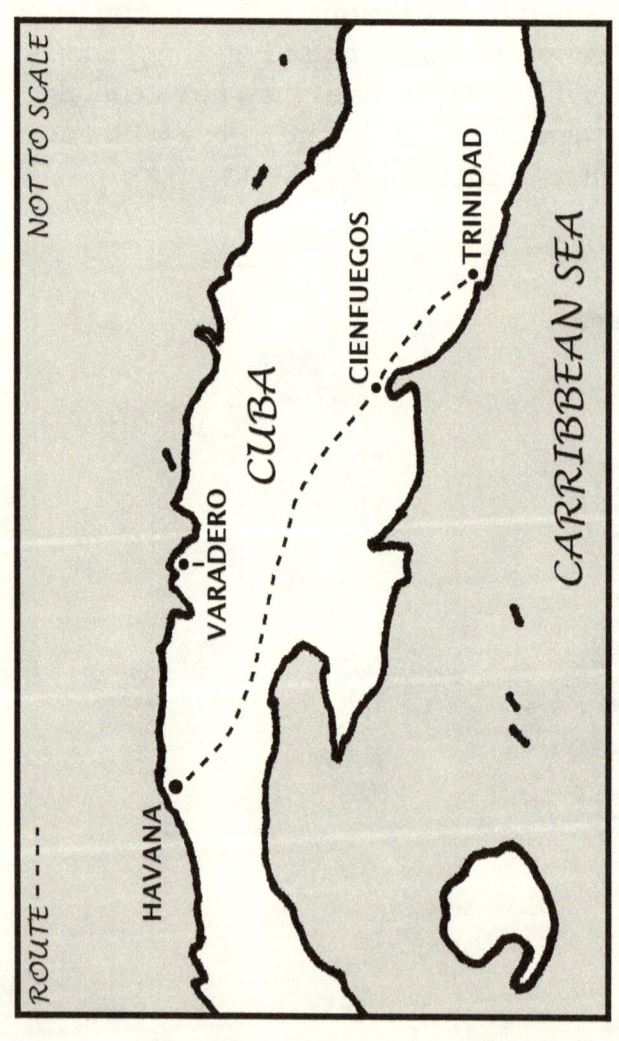

Cuba, early 2007

The decision to go to Cuba was based on conversations with friends who'd been there and enjoyed it, along with curiosity about a country that had a unique place in twentieth century history. The long-running standoff with the US seemed mildly farcical now though it was fair to say both sides indulged in rhetoric. Its beginnings went back to the days when the island was a playground for the rich and famous, something ended by the revolution in 1959. Allying with the Soviet Union, the invasion of The Bay of Pigs and the 1962 missile crisis had only entrenched the mistrust, leading to many years of posturing. However, there were rumours that Fidel Castro's health was fading and that age would inevitably catch up with the energetic firebrand. He had provisionally ceded power to his brother Raul, considered a reformist, and there were questions about how much this might change the country.

I spent the first week with my brother, a regular visitor on my travels, exploring Havana's familiar-looking streets and historic bars, before going to Varadero, a characterless strip of beach resorts on a long, narrow island some sixty miles east. Ending up there was an unfortunate accident, as we wanted to go to the historic south coast town of Trinidad, but hadn't been able to organise it so my brother could get back in time for his flight home. When he left I headed there, but was having a slothful morning, so arrived at the station in Havana too late to get a direct bus, instead hopping on one that would take me close enough to get a connection later in the afternoon. The journey to Cienfuegos, where I would change, was pleasantly bland, cutting southeast through the brown waste of harvested sugar cane fields. The bus arrived in good time, and I confirmed the next leg before finding a seat in the basic, crowded and uncomfortably hot station.

A few minutes later, the wiry man I'd spoken to at the information desk came over and quietly asked if I really wanted to wait, or whether I would prefer to take a taxi. His covert tone implied this wasn't going to be above-board, but he was friendly and seemed genuine, so there was no harm in having a conversation about it. I'd also just spent five hours on a bus that seemed detached from Cuba, and the chance to talk to someone from outside the government-run tourism industry was appealing. He offered to bring the driver inside, and soon after a large, goateed man in his mid twenties arrived. He also appeared sincere so we agreed a price, and he confirmed his probably wasn't a licensed cab when we conspired to meet in a parking area outside the station. He probably wasn't authorised to take tourists, but had just negotiated the fare in the middle of a busy bus station, so wasn't hiding too much. Nevertheless, I was happy with the arrangement; he made some money and I got to my destination quicker.

I walked to the rendezvous point and one of the classic US cars that Cuba abounds with pulled up. I can't remember the model but it definitely had a lot of character. It was battered, with multi-coloured panelling that gave it the air of a seasoned road hopper. I threw my pack on the back seat, jumped in and off we went. The first part of the journey was quiet as I think he was keen to get away from the city, but once outside he opened up a bit, and the usual assorted personal details were exchanged while Reggaeton blared from the stereo. As we travelled, I warmed to him. He was good fun and our small amounts of each other's languages didn't stop us communicating. We talked about the car and how it had belonged to his grandfather, then his father, and had now passed to him, the family vehicle, repaired and kept running for decades. Then he asked if I wanted to drive.

I gave my first instinctive answer – yes. We were on a quiet road, surrounded by fields, and it wouldn't do much harm to go a short distance. He pulled over, we changed places and he gave me some coaching on how to handle the car, basically heavy on the throttle to get the beast moving. The steering was a bit loose but I soon got used to it. He looked at me carefully and realising how pasty I looked, took his baseball cap off, put it on my head and laughed at how Cuban I looked. I wasn't convinced but it would do.

He started to enjoy not driving and let me stay behind the wheel longer than expected. It was late afternoon on a warm sunny day, and the smell of countryside that had been baked all day drifted through the open windows. A little later we passed through a village where a policeman stood at the main junction, but didn't pay any attention to us. Even so, this made both of us a little nervous and when we saw another policeman on a motorbike, we pulled over to switch back.

Soon after he stopped again and asked me to get in the back seat and pretend to sleep as there was a checkpoint coming up, probably the provincial border. I lay down and pulled the baseball cap down over my eyes, hoping that any policeman who looked in wouldn't notice my pale skin and ginger beard. This all seemed part of the day's adventure, even when we were stopped. Before getting out of the car he motioned for me to stay where I was, fake-sleeping on the back seat. At first the conversation was right next to the car but then the voices get further away, so I kept down, until a policeman opened the front passenger door and began searching through the small bag I'd left on the seat. He said something, which I took to be a question about whether it was mine or not. The way I said "Sí" was enough to prove my lack of Cuban roots. He smiled a gotcha smile and said, "Turista", which was unenthusiastically answered with the giveaway "Sí". He closed the door and walked away.

There seemed no reason to be horizontal anymore, so I sat up to see what was happening. There was a small wooden shelter on the other side of the road, where my driver stood with another policeman. The conversation became heated when they were joined by my discoverer, and I guessed this wasn't going to turn out well. A few minutes later, the first policeman came over and asked how much I'd agreed to pay. Not having discussed what we were supposed to say in this situation, I told the truth. He asked a couple of times to make sure before sauntering back across the road. Out of the corner of my eye I saw they were holding an ID card and writing a ticket, but they didn't seem to be interested in me. When we finally drove away, I asked him what had happened, and learnt he would have to pay a fine for transporting a tourist plus the fare we'd agreed. This was a massive amount for him and I couldn't help but feel guilty.

Understandably, the rest of the journey was gloomy, but I did manage to speak with him about the police and how they dealt with Cubans. His view was that they were out to get you, although it sounded like severe punishment rather than corruption; you'd be penalized in most European countries for operating an illegal taxi. More worrying was that he would now have a mark on his record and could expect a visit from his local police as well. I may not have understood all of the conversation, but it seemed that his greatest offence was not driving a tourist, but speaking to one at all. This only emphasised what I'd experienced since arriving, that your cash was the most important thing, and you should only mix with government approved Cubans. The quest for foreign currency was understandable and in many ways admirable, as it helped pay for schools, hospitals and the monthly rations that everyone received. Unfortunately, discouraging the ordinary citizen from mixing with outsiders seemed to indicate a lack of confidence in the much advertised revolution.

When we arrived in Trinidad I fished in my pocket and gave him all the money I had, thankfully enough to cover the fare, the fine and some more. There wasn't a lot else I could do at that time of the evening, there were no open banks and, because of the US embargo, no usable cash machines, so I wished him well and left the car, hoping he managed to get home without being hassled by the police.

My memories of the five or six weeks I spent in Cuba are good, the music being a personal highlight. People were fun and friendly, but most nights out involved a watching policeman at some point, and after my early episode on the road to Trinidad, I was probably over-conscious of the need to be cautious. Cubans lived in a different country to the one we visitors saw, and there was often a feeling that you were being hidden from the country's reality, which regrettably took some of the enjoyment out of what was otherwise a wonderful place to visit.

Travels with Checkpoints

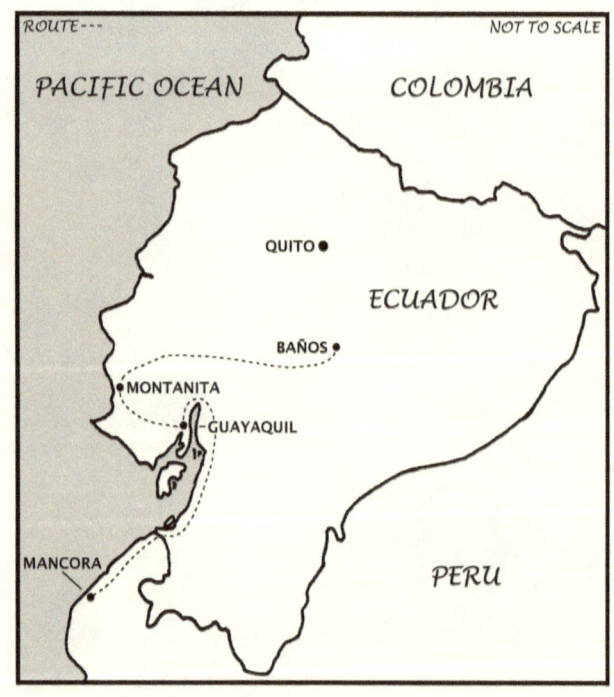

Ecuador, September 2010

In early September I left for a long trip around South America, flying into Quito, Ecuador's capital, where I spent a few days sleeping off jetlag and acclimatising to the altitude. I had to meet my brother in Lima, the capital of Peru, about four weeks later, so had time to get a flavour of the country, drifting around between the Andes and the Pacific coast, slowly getting used to enjoying the idea of a leisurely life for a few months.

Outside the tight sprawl of Quito, the country was more relaxed, and my amble took me to Baños, a laid back town in a steep mountain valley. I passed a few days enjoying the peace and people, before heading with some newfound friends to Montanita, a surf spot on the coast. We chanced upon a sweet little guesthouse near the beach and, having acquired the habit of doing very little, spent our days eating, drinking coffee and laughing.

It was wonderful but eventually we had to leave, in my case because it was only a week before I had to meet my brother, and

I was still a long way from Lima. My plan to gradually work my way down the north-western side of the continent had dissolved in an enjoyable mix of mild activity and laziness. My Swedish and English travelling companions and I decided to head for Guayaquil, Ecuador's most populous city, where we'd have a few hours wait before travelling on to Mancora, a beach town in northern Peru.

Just after five in the morning, the three of us hauled ourselves to the bus stop in Montanita. The journey was about four hours so we slept a bit more, arriving with plenty of time to catch the twelve thirty cross-border coach, which left from a small office a five minute walk away from the main terminal. We found it, located on a busy avenue, bought our tickets and checked our bags in.

We had two or three hours to waste so went back to the station to buy some food. As we sat outside the entrance, a girl from the US approached us and asked if we knew anything about a strike. She worked for an NGO somewhere outside the city and her boss had advised her to get back early so as not to get stuck. She seemed to be talking about transport problems, so we could only assure her that we'd just bought tickets to travel that day. She wandered off and we didn't think much about it as everything seemed normal. There were people coming and going, and the usual activity you'd expect in the transport hub of a large city.

We arrived back at the office about an hour before our bus was due to leave and heard a rumour that it was going to be delayed for three or four hours because of some "trouble" in Quito. This wasn't a disaster, just another opportunity to do nothing. When I went inside, people were watching the TV in the corner which was showing what looked like a demonstration. There were people burning tyres and the strap at the bottom of the screen suggested it might have been in Quito. I assumed our bus was held up there because the streets were blocked and it had taken longer to get out of the city than normal. My Spanish then didn't stretch past food and travel, so I could only look at the pictures and guess at what was going on.

Not long after this, everybody was called into the office and the manager made an announcement I didn't fully understand. Thankfully the woman next to me noticed my blank expression and offered to translate. She told us that the Peruvian border was closed because of the trouble in the capital and that we needed to come back the following morning at eleven to find out if it had reopened. She didn't offer too many details so we grabbed our bags and shuffled outside with everyone else. She then suggested we get off the streets, as the police were on strike and it wasn't safe. From her tone, it was obvious we should take her advice. Her father mentioned a hotel which we understood to be nearby, but when we asked if it was within walking distance he chuckled nervously and recommended we get a taxi. Throughout our conversation his wife had been looking around anxiously, and she finally said something to her husband and daughter which spurred them to rush off. This seemed to be the trend of the moment as when I looked around, almost everybody had fled.

That left eight of us – a mixed bunch of Europeans and North Americans – standing around apprehensively, but instinctively gathering together to get taxis to the hotel. The atmosphere started to feel strange and, even though it was midday, the eight lane boulevard outside the office was eerily quiet. We stood by the side of the road waiting as the occasional car passed us by, feeling like there was something we weren't being told. The tone of the manager's announcement and our translator's calm but firm insistence that we find a safe haven hadn't provided any details bar the fact that the police were on strike and the border was closed. This being all we knew, a feeling of danger exaggerated by a lack of knowledge enveloped us.

The only other people around now were the three men who worked in the bus office, the manager and two younger guys who worked the desk and luggage areas. When the first cab left, my two friends, me and a Latvian with a human sized suitcase waited by the empty road for what seemed like an unbearably long time, but finally another stopped and agreed to take us. The dour young driver wasn't sure where the hotel was, but he appeared not to be overly bothered about trying to find it. He made a phone call while we struggled to fit our backpacks in around the Latvian's suitcase, which took up most of the boot and eventually forced us to squeeze into the car with two of our bags. When we'd finally settled in, we travelled for about three seconds before the driver stopped and threw us out.

Our state of mind moved to bewildered as we took our hard fought luggage out and stood dazed by the side of the road. It turned out that the guys who worked in the bus office had been writing down the registration details of the car, something they must have done for the first one as well. The driver saw them and decided not to take us. This, the possibility that he may not have known where we were going and his phone call while we loaded our bags might not prove any ill intentions, but my heightened sense of insecurity could only bring all that evidence together and arrive at abduction, or worse. There were plenty of rumours about South American taxi drivers kidnapping and robbing people at gunpoint, so this wasn't an unreasonable conclusion, particularly during a police strike. We'll never know the real reason he wouldn't take us, and I'm happy to leave it that way.

The office staff ran over to us, and when the next cab stopped they had stern words with the driver, who seemed more trustworthy the moment he stepped out of his car. He was older, seemed to know the hotel we wanted to go to and had a more honourable manner than his predecessor. From what I understood he was told that his company would be called after we left, and although the whole situation still felt confusing and uncomfortable, we loaded up again as there was nothing else we could do. We'd had a helping hand and the only option available was to rely on this new improved driver.

On the way, our claustrophobic car glided through quiet, stifling streets, where most shops had already shut for the day. Peculiarly, there was no glass open onto the street; every frontage had a cage or metal shutters. At one junction, three men stood chatting and laughing, one holding a truncheon which he casually tapped against his leg, as if waiting for a reason to use it; those traffic lights took an age to change, leaving this prickly image embedded in our minds.

When we arrived the hotel was full and our driver was agitated, as I think he wanted to get home. The deserted streets of what was reputedly Ecuador's most dangerous city were no place for anyone that day. Two of the people in the other car spoke fluent Spanish, so became the de facto translators between taxis. This didn't make me feel any better as there were several conversations, translations and opinions going back and forth. Wedged in the back seat trying to work out what was going on only strengthened the baffled, isolated uncertainty.

Our driver offered to take us to the centre of town where there were several hotels and a better chance of finding space. A name was mentioned and the man with the human sized suitcase said he'd stayed there the night before. This sounded like a great idea, as where we were was a wasteland with a full hotel on it. A discussion about costs started but this wasn't a subject the occupants of our taxi had much interest in. We were somewhere in Guayaquil with nowhere to stay just after an unusual and possibly dangerous experience in the middle of a police strike – money wasn't on our minds. We took off in convoy towards the city, following the basic human instinct to find shelter.

We arrived about fifteen minutes later

and our driver went to the door of the hotel and shouted. A couple of guys appeared, hurriedly grabbed bags and helped us upstairs to the reception on the first floor. At the top of the stairs was a metal cage you had to be buzzed through, which made the place feel secure until you realised it was always there, even when the police were working. They had plenty of rooms available and we split ourselves across them, the three of us who'd spent the previous week together taking one room.

As we checked in, a kind looking man who worked at the hotel offered unsolicited advice about what we should and shouldn't do from that moment on. He recommended we didn't go out on the streets after three, as the private security guards who protected banks and shops with ancient shotguns would finish working then. Comments like this, while helpful in many ways, didn't reduce the anxiety we felt about the circumstances we found ourselves in – we weren't familiar with the city or Ecuador's political workings, so being told in a straightforward manner to only go outside when there were men with guns around didn't help us relax.

It was nearly two, so we dropped our bags and all of us bar the Latvian guy headed out to find some food. There was a rumour that the only place open was a nearby KFC, not my first choice, but not much of the day so far had been. As we left, the cage closed behind us and the main door downstairs was locked as well, never a good sign at that time of the afternoon. The streets were busier here but still uneasy, like the relative calm in the eye of a storm. Most shops were shut but there were armed guards outside some of them, a fact that was still reassuring and worrying in equal measure.

First on the outside world agenda was cash. As we had been due to cross a border, everyone had run down their supplies of paper money, ready to replenish on the other side. We found an ATM, and as each person tried to extract money the others, probably without realising, formed a human shield around them. That machine didn't work so we moved to another, which thankfully spat some dollar bills at us. We were near KFC but they'd closed their coop by then, so we had to find something else as time was marching on towards our three o' clock curfew. We spotted a small restaurant and headed in that direction.

About this time a demonstration came down the street carrying flags and chanting. There were only about thirty people but the street tensed as they strode aggressively past. I don't know what they were saying, but it didn't add any joy to the day. We got inside the restaurant and had an adequate meal, aware that it was probably our last chance to eat that day. As we walked back, we passed an open shop, stopping to pick up various snacks to keep us going through the evening. Back at base, the door was quickly opened and locked behind us before a large metal bar was placed across it as we advanced to the top of the stairs and through the cage. I started to feel more secure now as I didn't have any intention of leaving again that night, and the hotel seemed like the safest place we could hide from the still unknown dangers outside.

Earlier we'd given money to a guy who worked in the hotel so he could get us some rum, and after a mediocre doze, I joined the others in their room. As I walked through the door it was announced that things were worse than we'd thought or imagined. The TV news was reporting a coup attempt. The police had fired teargas at the president, who had been taken to a hospital, which was now under siege. We'd gone from being stuck for a night, to not really knowing when we'd be able to move on. We didn't have enough information to know what was going on outside and the situation could get worse or better, leaving us trapped for days, weeks or months. So we did the only thing we could at the time, drank some rum.

Some time later, another backpacker who'd been staying there arrived, and told us that he'd been out wandering the streets, watching protests and taking photos. He planned to go out again, but I wasn't going to go with him. All day, from the helpful woman at the bus office to the people in the hotel, my impression was that the streets weren't safe. Ecuadorians weren't going out, why would I? I was interested in the situation and the issues that caused it, and part of me would have loved to wander around seeing what Ecuadorian political instability looked like, but ignoring the advice of people who lived there every day somehow didn't feel right.

We all settled in and used someone's iPhone on an intermittent internet connection to send quick messages home saying we were safe. The unreliable communications only added to the sense of being cut off. When it was my turn, I'd received an email from a friend in England with a link to a report on the BBC News website about what was happening. There were descriptions of roadblocks across the country, occupation of the airport in Quito, plus looting and opportunistic muggings in Guayaquil. It was unclear who was attacking whom, or where the loyalties of the police and army lay, as factions from both seemed to be involved. I was no wiser when I finished reading, wondering whether we were stuck in the start of a civil war.

Later in the evening, when we'd run out of rum, we were told there was a shop open close to the hotel. We'd been confined to a windowless room for several hours by then and were going a little stir crazy, our only link to the outside world being a small balcony used for smoking where the smell of burning tyres would occasionally drift over us. We took our first steps outside, and the door was closed tight behind us leaving us standing warily on the deeply quiet street, a strange experience given we'd expected rioting everywhere. The shop wasn't far away and we bought some beer, which was passed through a gap in a metal cage. We went back and drank a bit more before somebody mentioned going out for food, an idea that gained momentum around the room, helped along by beer and rum. I declined and was asked if I was scared, but didn't feel the need to answer.

Everybody left apart from my original travelling companions from Montanita and me. We went back to our room in disbelief that anyone would choose to go further than the corner of our street. We learnt the next day that the hotel, in their positions as genuinely nice people, had tried to call a taxi and have them taken to a restaurant they knew would be safe. They'd refused and walked around the area we'd eaten in earlier. Thankfully they came back safely, but we hadn't considered it a risk worth taking. Having just read about looting and muggings, wandering aimlessly when almost everything had been shut at two seemed ridiculous.

I slept surprisingly well that night, waking next morning to the sound of helicopters, which could have meant anything. One of my friends went down to reception to find out what was going on, and a few minutes later I joined her as the owner's wife was trying to call the bus office for us. It took a few attempts but, when she got an answer, they said the border was open and the bus would leave at eleven thirty. We went out and grabbed a coffee and something to eat, discovering that the streets of Guayaquil had changed overnight, bustling like a city of that size should. The tensions of the previous day had disappeared and people were going about their business as if nothing had happened. The man who served us in the cafe refused to be drawn about the previous day, possibly embarrassed that we'd seen his country this way, or simply because it wasn't an extraordinary event.

The hotel called two cabs to take us to the coach office and we said our goodbyes to the staff. As I shook the hand of the man who had given us advice the previous day he solemnly said, "Suerte", a word I didn't understand at the time but found out a few minutes later meant "Good Luck". I wished he'd said it with a smile on his face. However our mood was definitely more upbeat as we headed out of the centre. There was quite a bit of hope that we would leave but until we crossed the border there would always be some doubt.

Everyone who'd been there the day before was waiting at the office to board, along with a few more who'd decided to get out while they could. Several police pickup trucks passed by, mostly filled with soldiers but occasionally some police as well. This was a good sign, as a highly visible presence was better than none. We got on the bus and hoped for no roadblocks. While the city had returned to normality, it didn't mean that everywhere had. Thankfully the journey to the border was uneventful, and about eight or nine that evening we arrived in Mancora where six of us got off the bus, went to a hostel by the beach, dumped our bags and went straight to the bar. I ended up staying another week there, enjoying the sun and sea before getting the last possible bus to Lima, refreshed after a draining twenty four hours in Guayaquil.

Travels with Checkpoints

Bolivia, December 2010

Following several weeks in Peru, I entered Bolivia near the breathtakingly magnificent Lake Titicaca, 3800 metres above sea level, yet still flanked by snowy peaks. Arriving at the sunny lakeside settlement of Copacabana, there was a noticeable change in atmosphere from what had seemed like excessively affected tourism on the other side of the border. The town and nearby Isla del Sol kept me captivated for a week or two before I managed to heave myself away to La Paz, the capital. This gentle introduction to the country was a good indication of what was to come as the variety of scenery was sublime, varying from the dry, high Altiplano to the humid jungle.

Following a month of travelling from the south-western salt flats and volcanic border with Chile, through the southern wine making region and north again to the bright city of Sucre, I arrived off a long night bus in Santa Cruz, situated at the edge of the Amazon basin. The country's most populous city considered itself more

Brazilian than Bolivian, and often made noises about independence. It was clean, tidy and the economic centre of one of the poorest countries in South America. Having been at high altitude for several months, breathing crisp mountain air, the sudden drop to the muggy jungle was overbearing. I found a place to sleep but tiredness, heat and the fierce argument between the owner of the hostel and somebody in my dorm – which included the unforgettable line, "You're a pirate, get out of my hostel!!" – made me grumpy with the whole town.

    I had developed a vague idea about travelling via train to near the border with Paraguay further south but, when I checked the timetable, discovered it only ran once a week, and the next one was the following day. The only other way into Paraguay was to take a thirty two hour coach to Asunción, the capital, and I wasn't in the mood for this. I had time so could do the journey in stages, stopping along the way to explore more of both countries. I bought a train ticket, spent the rest of the day in a hammock, and got a good night's sleep.

    The next afternoon I took my seat for the fourteen hour rattle down the eastern side of

Bolivia, arriving frazzled just before dawn in the south-eastern town of Villamontes. I took the first guesthouse that willingly opened its doors, a grubby spot where the manager joked about getting me a woman for the night, never a good start. It appeared to serve as a base for men working in the oil and gas industry, which had become the main source of income in the region and may have explained the instant offer of prostitution. However I was exhausted and it was cheap, just for one night and not the worst place I'd ever stayed. I wedged my bag against the door and slept for a couple of hours.

Later that morning I headed for the local bus company which ran a daily bus to Bolivian immigration, from where they said I could catch a bus on to the Paraguayan side. This would be important as there was a two hundred kilometre buffer zone separating the immigration posts of the two countries, a kind of extended no man's land. This arrangement stretched back to the 1930s when they had fought a war over the arid, inhospitable Chaco Boreal that stretched across the border. The conflict had ended in 1935 but there still seemed to be some localised paranoia in the border regions, and transport was sparse.

I spent the rest of the day wandering the town, one of the wealthiest looking I'd seen in Bolivia. The central square was immaculate, and walking a little further that morning would have found me a better class of accommodation than the room with the lumpy bed, stained sheets and see-through curtain. The following morning, after sleeping soundly and without incident, I caught the bus, a smallish vehicle with about twenty seats, most of which were filled when we left. There were some strange looks from my fellow passengers and I was asked where I was going. Answering Paraguay seemed to be accepted with a mildly perplexed look.

A brand new highway had been built linking Villamontes with Asunción, but for no obvious reason, it was blocked not far out of town. The driver took us off road through the Chaco, along sandy tracks that frequently threatened to swallow the wheels. The area away from the road was heavily forested and appeared to be two-toned; parched yellow from the ground to about two metres up, where the treetops were a grubby, yellowy-green colour.

Intermittently a farmhouse would appear and we'd stop to deliver boxes and bags to waiting families, the daily bus being their only lifeline. I realised we weren't travelling this dirt road for enjoyment, but wondered how people managed to survive. I'd seen no crops, some scrawny livestock and almost no water. There was a rainy season for six months of the year and vegetation on the hardy trees, even in the dry season, so maybe it was harsh but liveable.

About ninety minutes into the journey we reached an army base, the largest settlement I'd seen so far. Just after this was the immigration checkpoint where the bus stopped, and from here the road stretched off through the scrub towards Paraguay. The border post consisted of a bare brick building – a collection of walls with holes for windows, covered in places with black plastic sheeting. To the left of this were a couple of houses, one of which produced a man wearing a very new combat jacket with POLICE in large letters across the back, a pair of shorts and sandals. I handed over my passport and as he leafed through it, another man arrived wearing a pair of green trousers, a police belt complete with handcuffs, and a vest slightly stained with something. It appeared they were sharing the set of official clothes.

The first man asked me what transport I planned to use to get to Paraguay and seemed unimpressed with my bus answer. He explained that there was only one bus a day that arrived about four in the morning, and the only other way across was to try and hitch a ride with a passing truck. Both of these options were fine except that it was eleven in the morning and thirty five degrees, so it might have been a long, sweaty wait. I could have my passport stamped but there was no going back into Bolivia, I would have to stay there until I managed to get a lift. I wasn't convinced this was a good idea, as the bus started in Santa Cruz and might be full by the time it got to the border, plus there was no guaranteeing I could get a lift.

He counted something on his fingers and said I needed to pay one hundred and twenty Bolivianos. I'd been aware this might happen, as I'd extended my visa in Sucre ten days before. The entry stamp said "30 DIAS" and I had two of these which, in theory, meant sixty days, but had heard that border guards often claim this isn't a proper extension to try and force you to pay a fine for overstaying. While the amount of the fine was legal, the method was dubious. He was asking for about US$15-20, so it wasn't a massive amount from my budget, but I did object to a) paying a fine without having done anything wrong, and b) an amount of money that would make it worthwhile for him to pester everyone in the same situation.

I wasn't in the best position to argue though, being in the middle of nowhere with nothing but an army base and two oddly-dressed policemen for company. My only escape route was to get back on the bus, still parked outside, and go back to Villamontes, though that was something I wanted to avoid. I'd gotten this far and although it was my fault for not checking transport more carefully, I would have preferred to carry on into Paraguay if I could.

So I asked why, and that's when he became angry. He slammed my passport on the table and said I wouldn't be crossing that day. The sudden fury surprised me, and that was the only point I felt nervous; they could have held me there if they wished for whatever they wanted. I stood there silently until he calmed down, then said I'd wait and see if anything came through I could grab a lift with.

He softened his tone and offered to stamp my passport again, but I wasn't taking the chance of being stuck there with these two. I would be checked out of Bolivia but not into Paraguay. That guy who lived in Charles de Gaulle airport in Paris for seventeen years, not legally able to enter any country, came to mind. At least he had shops and a constant flow of people helping him out. I'd have to make do with begging from the occasional person passing through the border and playing immigration poker with my new chums to pass the time. I needed to get my passport back and stop discussing my options with them so refused, again saying I'd wait to see if any trucks came through. He handed me my passport and I wandered back to the bus, telling the confused driver I'd probably be coming back with him. His only comment was that I should try and cross somewhere else as there was not much transport where we were, something I think I'd already worked out.

About an hour later, the first guy, no longer wearing his police jacket, came past and asked again whether I wanted a stamp, as he was going for lunch. If a truck came through he wouldn't be around, but I hadn't seen any other vehicle, so I declined again as I'd already decided not to hang around. I was going back to Villamontes to take the route south to Argentina. He left, came back, one car came through from Paraguay, and I slept and sweltered in the heat. Now and again the policeman would emerge from his house, and we'd stare at each other with comic suspicion for a few moments, before he disappeared inside again. A fun afternoon was had by all.

Having sheltered from the sun for several hours we drove back through the Chaco, picking up people with dead goats they planned to sell in town. I booked into a better hotel for the night, feeling tired, dejected and fairly bored of Villamontes. Later that evening someone I met pointed out a few qualities of the local area, and I confess it sounded better than my less than objective, hastily developed view, but my mind was already made up.

The next morning I headed to the Argentine border. This turned out to be the easier option as it was a busy truck route, so there was no danger of getting stuck. I arrived at the Bolivian side and had a short discussion about Irish football with the policeman behind the desk. This seemed to smooth things over as when his colleague asked what to do with my passport, I tensed, but he said just stamp it and let him go. I walked over the bridge that separated the countries and waited two hours on the other side. It was close to Christmas and Argentineans were surging across the border to shop in their cheaper neighbour, clogging the customs area.

Once through I caught a bus to the nearest town with an inter-city station, and hopped on the next coach going east, with no particular plan in mind, which led me to sit at a remote crossroads with a friendly policeman for three hours, waiting for a night bus to take me to the city of Formosa. This was the nearest town to Asunción, and I planned to spend the night there before crossing the border. However, I hadn't known how busy everywhere got around this time, the equivalent of the northern hemisphere summer holiday, and every hotel was full, so I travelled south to Resistencia. It was here I made the decision to go to Puerto Iguazú, location of the impressive high-volume waterfalls in the northeast. I spent a week there, before eventually making it to Ciudad del Este, Paraguay, via Brazil, ten days later and a thousand kilometres southeast of where I'd originally planned. I'd skirted around the edge of the country, making an unintentional two thousand kilometre detour, mainly due to chronic disorganisation. I could have tried to plan a bit better I suppose, but where's the fun in that?

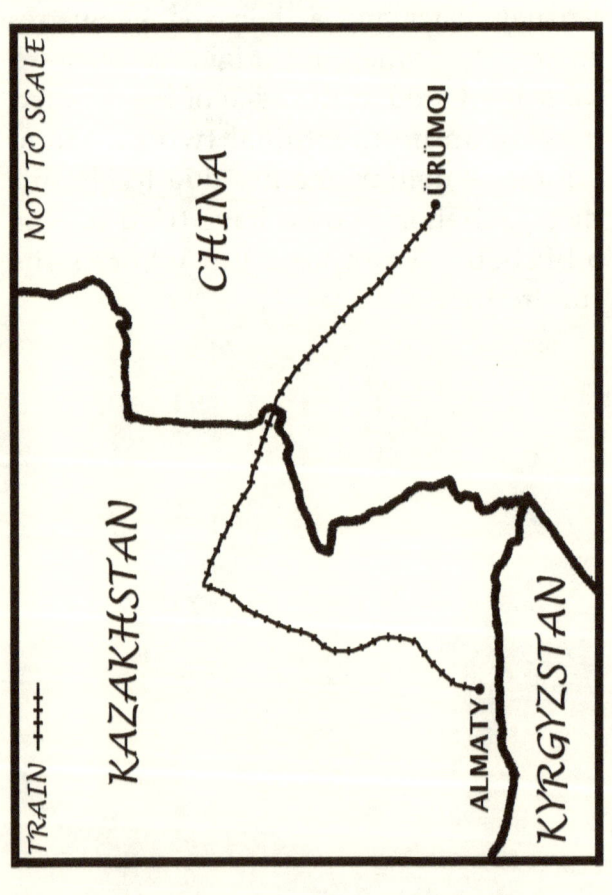

And Finally...

When I left Central Asia at the end of October 2005, I took a thirty six hour train journey from Almaty in Kazakhstan to Ürümqi in China's Uyghur Autonomous Region. In the weeks leading up to this, I'd been washing my clothes in a sink using a bar of clothes soap. The bother of this meant that I never washed all of the clothes in my bag, just a select few to get me through a few days at a time. The remaining items nestled at the bottom of my backpack, waiting for a time when a full wash could be done and, on the occasions they were disturbed, gave off a pungent aroma.

I booked a place in a four berth sleeper cabin from a surly woman at the main station in Almaty, who threw my ticket across the counter before storming out of the office. When I boarded I found I was sharing with three Kazakh women, whose natural Central Asian friendliness surfaced not long into the journey, once they'd gotten over their initial shock at the scruffy road-dusty Irishman in their midst.

It took about eighteen hours to get to the Kazakh border, where apparatchiks boarded the train. I was confident there would be no trouble as one of my travelling companions turned out to be the wife of somebody high up in the immigration department. Also, the Kazakh police and border guards were rumoured to be under orders not to bother foreigners, more and more of whom were coming to work the oil fields in the west of the country. In my ten days there this had seemed to be the case, but the policeman who first walked in had an arrogant gait, and my comfort level dropped somewhat as he fixed his eyes on me with a seedy grin. The lady whose husband worked for immigration politely asked for a private word, and everyone else filed out into the corridor, closing the door behind us. Less than a minute later he emerged sheepishly and scurried along the corridor, having no doubt had an explanation of why our compartment was not to be bothered.

We continued on to a yard where we stopped for several hours to make some changes to the train. The Soviets had built their railways with a different track gauge to almost everyone else, allegedly to stop neighbouring countries from being able to use them in an invasion. Each carriage had to be detached from its base and lifted up by crane. A new set of wheels were then slid underneath and the carriage reattached. The engineer in me found it interesting the first couple of times, the other four hours I spent buried in a book.

At the Chinese frontier, officials travelled efficiently through the train. My passport was stamped and then a young soldier who could speak English was called. He asked to see the luggage stored under the seats, and then for me to open my backpack. As he searched through the clothes at the bottom, the stench that filled that tiny space made everyone wince. There were sharp intakes of breath cut short by the realisation that more of the unwashed smell got up your nose and in your mouth. I was quickly and politely told to close my bag and the two Chinese guards who'd been standing near the door moved quickly on.

It occurred to me at the time that maybe this was what I'd been searching for, a way to stop anybody bothering me in any country. A skunk-like defence mechanism designed to repulse any border guard or policeman. However, given the reaction of the rest of the cabin, it might not be my first choice.

Acknowledgements

I'm exceptionally grateful to every person I met along the way who helped when a lack of local knowledge could have proved dangerous.

Thanks to all those who helped with proofreading, particularly my mother Mella, sister Ailbhe, Fi and Charlotte, who checked my structure and grammar across several versions.

www.ingramcontent.com/pod-product-compliance
Lightning Source LLC
Chambersburg PA
CBHW022020290426
44109CB00015B/1252